How Fast Fashion Changed the World

Stephanie Feldstein

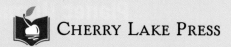
CHERRY LAKE PRESS

Published in the United States of America by Cherry Lake Publishing Group
Ann Arbor, Michigan
www.cherrylakepublishing.com

Reading Adviser: Beth Walker Gambro, MS, Ed., Reading Consultant, Yorkville, IL

Photo Credits: © Milan Ilic Photographer/Shutterstock, cover; © Karol Kozlowski/Shutterstock, 4; © Larina Marina/Shutterstock, 6; Internet Archive Book Images, No restrictions, via Wikimedia Commons, 9; © nito/Shutterstock, 10; © Mrs_ya/Shutterstock, 11; © Fardous Hasan Pranto/Shutterstock, 12; © triocean/Shutterstock, 13; © Luoxi/Shutterstock, 14; © lenetstan/Shutterstock, 15; © New Africa/Shutterstock, 16; © wee dezign/Shutterstock, 17; © P.Cartwright/Shutterstock, 19, © wonderisland/Shutterstock, 20; © 1000 Words/Shutterstock, 21; © pcruciatti/Shutterstock, 22; © Stanislav71/Shutterstock, 25; © Monkey Business Images/Shutterstock, 26; © artjazz/Shutterstock, 27; © dutchcows/Shutterstock, 28; © Vera Prokhorova/Shutterstock, 29; © NatalyaBond/Shutterstock, 30

Cherry Lake Press is an imprint of Cherry Lake Publishing Group.

Library of Congress Cataloging-in-Publication Data

Names: Feldstein, Stephanie, author.
Title: How fast fashion changed the world / Written by: Stephanie Feldstein.
Description: Ann Arbor, Michigan : Cherry Lake Publishing, 2024. | Series: Planet human | Audience: Grades 4-6 | Summary: "The fast fashion industry has profoundly impacted our world. The Planet Human series breaks down the human impact on the environment over time and around the globe. Each title presents important high-interest natural science nonfiction content with global relevance"— Provided by publisher.
Identifiers: LCCN 2023035099 | ISBN 9781668939079 (paperback) | ISBN 9781668938034 (hardcover) | ISBN 9781668940419 (ebook) | ISBN 9781668941768 (pdf)
Subjects: LCSH: Clothing trade—Juvenile literature.
Classification: LCC HD9940.A2 F45 2024 | DDC 687.068/8—dc23/eng/20230808
LC record available at https://lccn.loc.gov/2023035099

Cherry Lake Publishing Group would like to acknowledge the work of the Partnership for 21st Century Learning, a Network of Battelle for Kids. Please visit Battelle for Kids online for more information.

Printed in the United States of America

Note from publisher: Websites change regularly, and their future contents are outside of our control. Supervise children when conducting any recommended online searches for extended learning opportunities.

Stephanie Feldstein works at the Center for Biological Diversity. She advocates to protect wildlife and helps people understand how humans impact nature. She lives in the woods in the Pacific Northwest with her rescued dogs and cats. She loves to hike and explore wild places.

CONTENTS

Introduction

A Mountain of Clothes

The Atacama Desert is one of the driest deserts on Earth. It's in Chile. But it looks like Mars. Scientists study the desert to learn what life might be like on other planets. There's no other place like it. But this special landscape has changed. Now it has mountains of clothes.

Giant piles of clothes stretch across the desert. People search through the clothes for things to resell or recycle. But the mountains are too big. They keep growing. At least 39,000 tons of discarded clothes are added each year.

Clothes are part of everyday life. They protect us from the weather. They keep us comfortable. You can't go very many places without them. But **fast fashion** creates a huge amount of waste. It harms workers and the environment.

A Giant Industry

Fashion is one of the biggest industries in the world. Hundreds of millions of people work to make and sell clothes.

All of this production uses a lot of material. The material comes from plants, animals, and **fossil fuels**. Turning material into clothes creates **pollution**. It worsens **climate change**.

More than 100 million tons of clothing are thrown away each year. Almost all of it winds up as trash. Less than 1 percent of old clothing gets recycled into new clothes. But clothing doesn't have to be thrown away. It can be repaired. It can be made to last longer.

Fast fashion is clothing made cheaply and quickly. It's made for people to buy lots of clothes in places like the United States and Europe. Then the clothes are thrown away for the next **trend**. The waste is sent to countries across South America, Asia, and Africa. The clothes become mountains of garbage.

Human **industry** has changed the face of the planet. More than 8 billion people live on Earth. People are living longer. We're healthier than ever. But everything we use or buy comes at a cost. Human industry uses natural resources that wildlife needs. It creates pollution and waste. It can affect human health, too. Our industries put a lot of pressure on nature. The most pressure comes from wealthy countries like the United States.

We need a healthy planet to survive. We need clean air and safe water. We need **ecosystems** with lots of different wildlife. Industries like fast fashion have a huge impact on the world. But there's a better way. We can have fashion that's good for people and the planet.

CHAPTER 1

The History of Fast Fashion

Fashion trends have been around since ancient times. But only wealthy people could afford colorful styles. Clothes were made by hand. They had to last a long time. Fabrics were made from natural fibers like wool, linen, and cotton.

The sewing machine was invented in the 1800s. Clothes became easier to make. They became less expensive. They started to be made in factories.

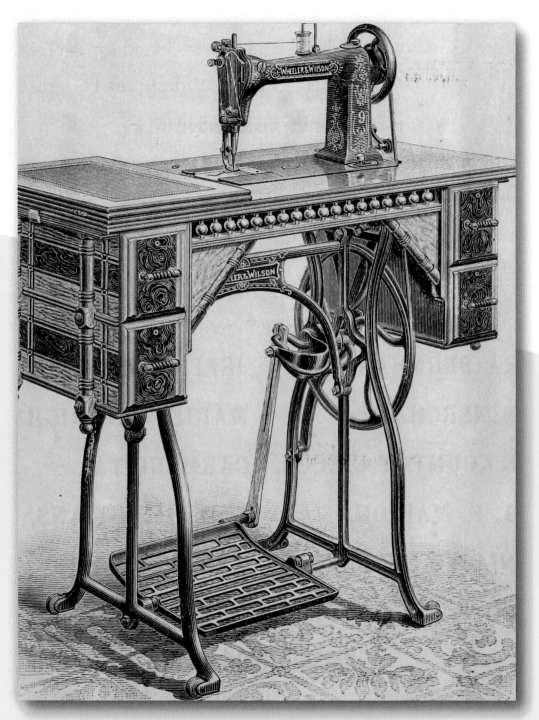

When the sewing machine was invented, it cut down the amount of time
it took to make each piece of clothing. It was a game-changer!

Styles became simpler during World War II (1939–1945). Many people wore uniforms. Clothes were mass-produced. **Mass production** is when factories make a lot of the same product. It's usually made by machines instead of by hand.

Clothes made from **synthetic** fibers became popular after the war. Synthetic fibers are not made of natural materials. They don't biodegrade or naturally break down in the environment. But synthetic clothes are easy to care for. They don't shrink in the wash. They don't wrinkle or tear as easily. They're less expensive.

Fashion and Human Health

The fashion industry uses a lot of **toxic** chemicals. One-fifth of all **insecticides** used in the world are used on cotton plants. Insecticides are a type of poison. They're made to kill bugs that eat crops. Similar insecticides are used to produce wool and leather from sheep and cows. They're put on the plants fed to the sheep and cows.

Clothing factories use many kinds of chemicals. They're used to make fabrics less likely to burn. Some make materials like wool machine-washable. Some dyes used to make colorful fabric are toxic.

These chemicals can make workers very sick. They can have trouble breathing. They can get cancer and other illnesses. Some of these chemicals get into the air and water. Communities near factories and farms can get sick, too.

Many fast-fashion brands sold in the United States have large clothing factories overseas.

Prêt-à-porter clothing, or ready-to-wear clothing, was first developed in major haute couture fashion houses. It was the first time clothing could be mass-produced in standard sizes. It lowered the cost for consumers.

By the 1960s, people wanted more inexpensive, stylish choices. Trends began to move very quickly. Fashion brands raced to keep up with demand.

Over the next few decades, people bought lots of cheap clothes. More big factories were built. Many were built in less-developed countries. They made clothes for the United States and Europe. Workers were paid very little. They worked in dangerous conditions. This is how most fast fashion is still made today.

The term "fast fashion" was first used in the 1990s. The *New York Times* used it to describe a company that was new to the city. The company said it only took 15 days for a new style to go from design to the store.

OUR DIRTY LAUNDRY

Microfiber pollution comes from clothing when it's washed. Tiny pieces of fiber get into the environment. Each load of laundry can release 700,000 microfibers. They're so small that they're easily eaten by wild animals. They can make the animals sick. Many microfibers are synthetic materials. They fill up the animals so they can't eat real food.

Washing clothes less often can reduce microfiber pollution. It also saves water. And it can help clothes last longer. Jeans can be worn 10 times before going in the laundry unless they get dirty.

Fast fashion companies are full of designers. These designers look at popular fashions and try to re-create them.

On average, every woman in the United States has 103 items of clothing in her closet.

Online shopping has made all kinds of fashion more accessible to consumers: from fast fashion to more sustainable fashion.

Production has only become faster. New styles are created at dizzying speeds. Some brands upload 1,000 styles a day to their websites. Fashion used to have just two seasons. People bought lighter, colorful clothes for spring and summer. Warm, cozy styles were for fall and winter. Now there are as many as 52 "micro-seasons."

CHAPTER 2

The Environmental Cost of Fast Fashion

Fossil fuels are used to make synthetic fibers. Almost two-thirds of all fibers made today are synthetic. Fossil fuels cause climate change. They also cause air, land, and water pollution.

Many fibers come from plants and animals. Chemicals are used to keep bugs and weeds away from crops. Forests are cut down to make room for farms. Industrial farming causes climate change, too.

Climate change makes it harder for wildlife to find food. Warmer temperatures make it harder for wild animals and insects to survive. They're killed by oil spills. They're poisoned by chemicals put on crops. They lose their homes

Trees are often cut down to make way for cotton, hemp, and flax crops, which are heavily used in fiber production for fast fashion.

Every year, more than 1.2 trillion gallons (4.5 trillion liters) of groundwater, untreated sewage, and waste from various industries is dumped into U.S. water.

when forests and grasslands are turned into farms. Their homes are ruined by oil drilling and pollution. All of these threats are part of fast fashion.

Fashion uses enough water to fill 37 million Olympic swimming pools a year. Most of that water is polluted. The polluted water is often dumped into rivers or streams. It turns the water into sludge. It kills wildlife. It makes the water unhealthy to use or drink.

More clothing is made than people will buy. Almost one out of three pieces of clothing are never sold. And making clothes quickly wastes fabric. Most of the extra clothing

Changemaker: Mikaela Loach

Mikaela Loach is a **climate justice** activist. She speaks out for those most harmed by climate change. She speaks out for policies that treat people fairly. She also loves fashion. She knows fashion and climate justice are related.

Loach learned how industries like fashion hurt people and the planet. She made changes to her own life. She stopped buying new clothes made in the fast fashion industry. But she knew bigger change was needed, too. She became an activist.

In 2021, Loach hosted *ReDress the Future*. This TV series is about redesigning the fashion industry. Loach shares ways people can stop buying new clothes. She talks to designers using materials that are better for Earth.

Loach helps other people become activists. She uses her writing, podcast, and social media accounts. She helps people connect with the issues. She shows how everyone can take action. She shares ways that others can quit fast fashion, too.

Many luxury brands have been around for a long time.
Chanel, Gucci, Prada, and Dior are some examples.

and fabric scraps wind up in the trash. More than 11 million tons of fabric goes to U.S. landfills each year. Most of those clothes are made of synthetic fibers. They don't biodegrade.

Expensive clothes aren't always better. They're made to last longer. But they use a lot of the same harmful materials. Luxury brands also make more clothes than they can sell. The whole fashion industry needs to change. They can slow down trends. And they can use fewer harmful materials.

TEXTILE INDUSTRY INSIGHT

Fabrics are also called **textiles**. Textiles are used for more than just clothes. They're all around your home. Bedding, curtains, furniture, and rugs are made of fibers. These fibers are just like those made into jeans or sweaters. Most of them are grown using pesticides. They're made from plants or animals. Or they're made from fossil fuels. They're treated with chemicals. They're dyed to be colorful.

Changing fashion helps change other parts of the textile industry. Less harmful materials used in clothes can be used for other things, too.

Setting New Trends

The fashion industry needs to slow down. Fast fashion companies keep using harmful fabrics. They want to keep making clothes as cheaply as possible. But we can make clothes in less harmful ways. And we can change the way we buy clothes.

Some companies help people care for their clothes so they last longer. They offer repair services. They make videos about how to keep clothes from wearing out. Some companies buy back used clothing. Then they resell it so people don't have to buy new. This helps reduce the new clothes being made.

Cheap fast fashion isn't as trendy as it used to be. Secondhand stores are becoming more popular. Social media videos show ways to use what's already in your closet. People are learning to be conscious consumers.

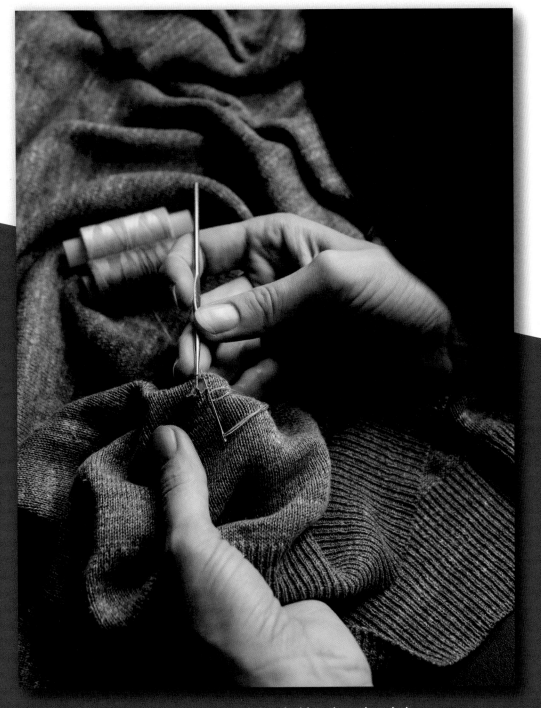

Many people are learning how to mend the clothing they already have.

Shoppers are making more conscious choices about the clothes they choose to buy.

They're thinking twice before shopping. This helps the planet and saves money.

Making and buying less clothes is important. But what clothes are made of also matters. Many clothing materials are better for the environment.

Recycled fibers use less water. They don't need more fossil fuels or animals to make them. They save fabric.

Organic cotton isn't grown with toxic chemicals. Fabrics like linen and hemp come from plants that use less water. People are finding new ways to use natural materials. Banana plants and orange peels are being used to make fabric.

HIGHER STANDARDS

The fast fashion industry doesn't pay for its pollution. It doesn't pay for its impact on the climate. It doesn't pay for how it treats workers.

Leaders are trying to change that. They're working to pass new fashion laws in New York and countries of the European Union. The laws would make the industry meet environmental goals. They would improve working conditions. The industry would have to pay for the harm it causes. Companies would have to change how they make clothes.

The Future of Fashion

Leather has been used for thousands of years. But today, it's part of a giant, destructive industry. More than 1.5 billion cattle are raised each year. Cows need a lot of food and water. They're killed to make beef and leather. Turning their skins into fabric often uses toxic chemicals. It creates a lot of pollution. Cows also trample the land. They worsen climate change by producing large amounts of methane gas. Methane hurts the atmosphere.

Leather clothing doesn't have to come from cattle. Companies are using technology to make fabrics from plants that look and feel like leather. No animals are harmed to make it. A good way to make sure leather alternatives are not bad for the environment is to research the company. Research the fabrics they are using. Knowledge is power!

Rather than shopping for new clothes, many people are being more sustainable by swapping used clothes with friends.

New fabrics are being invented all the time. Some are made from wood without deforestation. The fibers can biodegrade. Some are made in labs. They're made from natural materials. They're designed not to cause microfiber pollution. These new fabrics are better for the planet.

Many shoppers are demanding better clothes. They want materials that won't harm the environment. They want fewer clothes that will last longer. When people change how they shop, it makes the industry change, too.

Activity

Shop Your Closet

We often buy new clothes when we don't really need to. We're tempted by back-to-school sales. We want to keep up with changing styles. But every new outfit has an impact on the planet.

The best way to stop fast fashion is to use what you already have. Shopping your closet can give your clothes new life. Here are three ways to do it:

1. **Get organized.** Organizing your closet can help you find clothes you forgot you had. It can help you see your clothes in a new light. Organize your closet so things are easy to find. You can organize by type of clothing or color.

2. **Style new outfits.** Think about fast fashion outlets that you've seen in stores or online. Choose three different looks. Mix and match what you already have to create similar outfits.

3. **Give your clothes a makeover.** Many of us have clothes we don't wear very much. They might have a hole or stain. Or we might not like the style anymore. Choose three pieces of clothing and think about how you can give them new life.

If you do need to get new clothes, be a conscious consumer. Ask yourself questions before you buy: Is there a choice that's better for the planet? Could I find it at a secondhand shop?

Learn More

Books

Delisle, Raina. *Fashion Forward: Striving for Sustainable Style.* Victoria, BC: Orca Book Publishers, 2022.

Fontichiaro, Kristin. *Hacking Fashion: Denim.* Ann Arbor, MI: Cherry Lake Publishing, 2017.

Fontichiaro, Kristin. *Hacking Fashion: T-Shirts.* Ann Arbor, MI: Cherry Lake Publishing, 2015.

ReDress the Future. TV series hosted by Mikaela Loach, 2021.

Thomas, Dana. *Fashionopolis: The Secrets Behind the Clothes We Wear.* New York, NY: Dial Books, 2022.

On the Web

With an adult, learn more online with these suggested searches.

"6 Interesting Facts About Fast Fashion for Kids" — kids.earth.org

"How Does Fast Fashion Affect the Environment?" — kids.earth.org

"Is Your Fleece Jacket Polluting the Ocean?" Video — Above the Noise/KQED

Glossary

climate change (KLIYE-muht CHAYNJ) changes in weather, temperatures, and other natural conditions over time

climate justice (KLIYE-muht JUH-stuhs) the fair treatment of all people in policies that address climate change and the systems that cause it

conscious consumers (KAHN-shuhs kuhn-SOO-muhrz) people who are thoughtful about the impact of what they buy

ecosystems (EE-koh-sih-stuhmz) places where plants, animals, and the environment rely on each other

fast fashion (FAST FASH-uhn) clothing made cheaply and quickly, causing harm to people and the planet

fossil fuels (FAH-suhl FYOOLZ) fuels like oil, gas, and coal that come from the remains of plants and animals and are burned for energy

industry (IN-duh-stree) all the companies that make and sell a kind of product or service

insecticides (in-SEK-tuh-siedz) toxic chemicals made to kill bugs

mass production (MAS pruh-DUHK-shuhn) the process of making a large amount of the same product, usually by machines

microfiber pollution (MIYE-kroh-fiye-buhr puh-LOO-shuhn) tiny pieces of fabric that come off clothes during washing and get into the environment

pollution (puh-LOO-shuhn) harmful materials released into the environment

synthetic (sin-THEH-tik) not made from natural materials

textiles (TEK-stiyelz) fabric goods

toxic (TAHK-sik) something that is harmful or poisonous

trend (TREND) something that is popular for a certain period of time

Index